MIDLOTHIAN PUBLIC LIBRARY

3 1614 00195 8710

P9-CCG-882

OUR BILL OF RIGHTS

PLEAD THE FIFTH

A LOOK AT THE FIFTH AMENDMENT

JENNA TOLLI

MIDLOTHIAN PUBLIC LIBRARY
14701 S. KENTON AVENUE
MIDLOTHIAN, IL 60445

PowerKiDS
press.

NEW YORK

JUV
342.73
TOU

Published in 2019 by The Rosen Publishing Group, Inc.
29 East 21st Street, New York, NY 10010

Copyright © 2019 by The Rosen Publishing Group, Inc.

All rights reserved. No part of this book may be reproduced in any form without permission in writing from the publisher, except by a reviewer.

Editor: Sharon Gleason
Book Design: Rachel Rising

Photo Credits: Cover Stephen Coburn/Shutterstock.com; Cover, pp. 1, 3, 4, 5, 6, 7, 8, 9, 10, 11, 12, 13, 14, 16, 18, 20, 22, 24, 25, 26, 28, 29, 30, 31, 32 (background) Flas100/Shutterstock.com; Cover, pp. 1, 3, 4, 5, 6, 7, 8, 9, 10, 11, 12, 13, 14, 16, 18, 20, 22, 24, 25, 26, 28, 29, 30, 31, 32 (background) Mad Dog/Shutterstock.com; p. 4 larry1235/ Shutterstock.com; p. 5 SuperStock/SuperStock/Getty Images; p. 7 Jurgen Vogt/The Image Bank/Getty Images; p. 8 zimmytws/Shutterstock.com; pp. 9, 15 wavebreakmedia/Shutterstock.com; pp. 11, 17, 24 sirtravelalot/ Shutterstock.com; pp. 12, 16, 18, 28 (arrow) Forest Foxy/Shutterstock.com; p. 13 aerogondo2/Shutterstock.com; p. 19 Cameron Whitman/Shutterstock.com; p. 21 Tim Roberts Photography/Shutterstock.com; p. 21 (insert) Tom Grundy/Shutterstock.com; p. 23 Rich Koele/Shutterstock.com; p. 25 Boston Globe/Contributor/Getty Images; p. 27 Spencer Platt/Getty Images News/Getty Images; p. 29 selinofoto/Shutterstock.com; p. 30 Andrii Bielov/ Shutterstock.com.

Library of Congress Cataloging-in-Publication Data

Names: Tolli, Jenna, author.
Title: Plead the fifth : a look at the fifth amendment / Jenna Tolli.
Description: New York : PowerKids Press, 2019. | Series: Our Bill of Rights |
   Includes index.
Identifiers: LCCN 2018019918| ISBN 9781538343029 (library bound) | ISBN
   9781538343005 (pbk.) | ISBN 9781538343012 (6 pack)
Subjects: LCSH: United States. Constitution. 5th Amendment--Juvenile
   literature. | Due process of law--United States--Juvenile literature. |
   Self-incrimination--United States--Juvenile literature. | Eminent
   domain--United States--Juvenile literature.
Classification: LCC KF4558 5th .T65 2019 | DDC 345.73/056--dc23
LC record available at https://lccn.loc.gov/2018019918

Manufactured in the United States of America

CPSIA Compliance Information: Batch #CWPK19 For further information contact Rosen Publishing, New York, New York at 1-800-237-9932.

CONTENTS

PROTECTING INDIVIDUAL RIGHTS

The U.S. Constitution went into effect in 1789. It serves as the supreme law of the United States. It promises certain basic rights to American citizens and creates a system of checks and balances to prevent the government from becoming too powerful. However, many citizens and state representatives believed the Constitution didn't do enough to protect their individual rights. They also felt it didn't put clear limits on the government's power.

State representatives met in Philadelphia, Pennsylvania, in 1787 to create the Constitution. This was called the Constitutional Convention.

James Madison, a representative from Virginia, reviewed changes suggested by the states. He used their suggestions to create a list of changes to the Constitution that would protect the rights of citizens.

NEED FOR A BILL OF RIGHTS

Madison proposed a list of amendments, or changes, to the Constitution that would give Americans specific freedoms and rights. The list was influenced by the Virginia Declaration of Rights, which protected individual rights and explained the role, or place, of government. George Mason, an influential politician, wrote the Virginia Declaration of Rights in 1776.

Madison suggested a number of amendments to Congress. Twelve of these amendments were approved and sent to the states to be ratified, or approved. Only 10 of the amendments were ratified by enough states. These amendments became known as the Bill of Rights.

KNOW YOUR RIGHTS!

The Constitution, Bill of Rights, and Declaration of Independence are known together as the Charters of Freedom. These **documents** are very important to American history.

CHANGING THE CONSTITUTION

The fifth article of the Constitution explains the two steps for an amendment to be added to the Constitution. First, Congress must vote to propose the amendment (or two-thirds of the states must call for a constitutional convention). The amendment must be ratified by three-fourths of the states. If so, it's added to the Constitution. It's important that these groups review the amendment to make sure it's a fair and just addition to the Constitution.

The original Bill of Rights is on display at the National Archives Building in Washington, D.C., along with other historical documents.

FIFTH AMENDMENT

Each of the 10 amendments in the Bill of Rights serves an important purpose. The Fifth Amendment protects the rights of people who have been accused of a crime. It also protects a person's life, liberty, and property. This amendment is most well known as the source of the term "plead the Fifth," but it also includes other protections for citizens' individual rights.

5th Amendment

When someone is accused of a crime, it doesn't necessarily mean that person is guilty. The Fifth Amendment helps protect the rights of citizens and allows them an opportunity to prove their innocence in court.

There are five clauses, or distinct parts, that make up the Fifth Amendment. Each clause is a separate section of the amendment that explains how individual rights are protected in the federal justice system.

Overall, the Fifth Amendment limits the power that the government can have over American citizens and provides rights to citizens when they're accused of a crime.

GRAND JURY

"No person shall be held to answer for a capital, or otherwise **infamous** crime, unless on a **presentment** or **indictment** of a Grand Jury, except in cases arising in the land or naval forces, or in the **Militia**, when in actual service in time of war or public danger…"

The beginning of the Fifth Amendment protects citizens from unfair charges and **prosecution** from the federal government by using grand juries.

A grand jury is made up of a group of citizens from the community. A grand jury doesn't hear a trial or decide whether the defendant—a person accused of committing a crime—is guilty. Instead, grand jury members hear evidence and then decide if there is **probable cause** to believe that the accused person may have committed the crime. If they determine there's enough evidence, the case will go to trial.

KNOW YOUR RIGHTS!

Grand juries are only used for the most serious crimes, especially in cases that could result in the death penalty if the defendant is found guilty.

MILITARY EXCEPTION

There's an exception for the right to a grand jury for military members in times of war. These cases are handled in military courts, which have a different set of rules to handle serious crimes for people in the military.

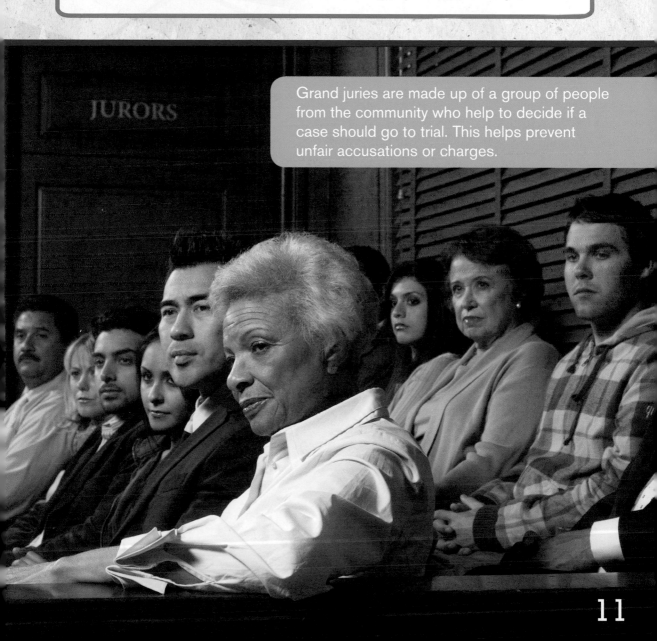

JURORS

Grand juries are made up of a group of people from the community who help to decide if a case should go to trial. This helps prevent unfair accusations or charges.

DOUBLE JEOPARDY

"…nor shall any person be subject for the same offence to be twice put in **jeopardy** of life or limb…"

This section of the Fifth Amendment protects people accused of crimes from being put on trial more than once for the same crime, which is called double jeopardy. It also protects someone from receiving multiple punishments for the same crime.

When someone goes to trial, the judge or jury decides whether that person is guilty of the crime they're charged with. Once that decision is made, in general, that person can't be called back to federal court to go on trial again for the same offense. This means someone can't be put on trial more than once for the same crime even if the government or prosecution isn't satisfied with the **verdict**.

What happens if someone breaks a state law and a federal law at the same time? Double jeopardy doesn't apply between federal and state courts, so it's possible someone could be charged in both courts for the same act.

MULTIPLE CHARGES

Just because a person is found innocent of a certain crime doesn't mean they're off the hook. A person can be found guilty for another crime that occurred at the same time. For example, if someone steals a car and robs a bank, that person could be charged with both crimes. If the person is found innocent of the theft of the car, they can still be found guilty of the robbery. Double jeopardy only applies to a single criminal charge.

SELF-INCRIMINATION

"…nor shall be compelled in any criminal case to be a witness against himself…"

The next section of the Fifth Amendment is called the self-incrimination clause. Self-incrimination is when someone provides information that could be used against them as evidence of a crime.

This section gives citizens the right to decide whether they'll answer questions during a trial if their answers could provide evidence against them. This is a choice for both individuals on trial and for witnesses who give **testimony**.

The terms "I plead the Fifth" or "I take the Fifth" come from this section of the Fifth Amendment. When people choose to "plead the Fifth," they've decided to **invoke** their Fifth Amendment right to avoid giving testimony that could incriminate them, or make them appear guilty.

KNOW YOUR RIGHTS!

The self-incrimination clause protects a person from their own words, but physical evidence, such as fingerprints, isn't protected under the Fifth Amendment.

Before people testify in court, they take an oath to swear they will tell the truth. The Fifth Amendment gives people the right to refuse to answer a question, which doesn't break this oath.

WHY PLEAD THE FIFTH?

There are different reasons someone may choose to "plead the Fifth" during testimony. For example, some defendants may not want to answer the prosecutor's questions because they're actually guilty of the crime and don't want to incriminate themselves.

It's also possible that the person isn't guilty but doesn't want to answer questions in court for other reasons. For example, someone may want to protect another person, or they may want to avoid admitting to another crime that the court doesn't already know about.

In the Supreme Court case *Griffin v. California* (1965), the court ruled that prosecutors and judges can't tell the jury that someone's decision to remain silent during questioning is evidence that they're guilty.

When a person accused of a crime decides to testify in court, they can't choose to answer some questions but not others.

DUE PROCESS

"…nor be **deprived** of life, liberty, or property, without due process of law…"

The due process clause in the Fifth Amendment means that certain rules and procedures must be followed before the government can take away someone's life, liberty, or property. This is meant to make sure that everyone gets fair treatment and that laws are applied equally to all people.

The protection of due process includes the right for a defendant to have advance notice of the trial, to appear in court, and to have the opportunity to be heard in court. This gives defendants enough time to prepare their arguments for the court and the ability to explain their side of the story before the verdict is made.

The Supreme Court building has the words "equal justice under law" engraved on it. The right to fair treatment is promised in the Constitution.

TAKINGS CLAUSE

"…nor shall private property be taken for public use, without just compensation."

The last clause in the Fifth Amendment explains the rights of individuals when the government is interested in taking over their private property for public use. It also addresses the rights of the government to take the property in certain cases.

The government holds what's called "eminent domain," which grants it the power to take over private property. In these cases, the government's required to prove the property is needed for public use. It also needs to give the original owner "just compensation," which is a fair price for the property.

The government may choose to take over private property to create parks, highways, or buildings that can be used by the public.

KNOW YOUR RIGHTS!

If the government wants to take over a property but the owner doesn't want to give it up, it's possible to challenge the case. The owner has the right to bring the case to court.

U. S. GOVERNMENT PROPERTY
— NO —
TRESPASSING
CLOSED TO THE PUBLIC

The government could take over someone's property if the land is needed to serve the public, such as for transportation.

ADDING AMENDMENTS

There have been many changes since the Bill of Rights was put into effect more than 200 years ago. Since the Bill of Rights was ratified in 1791, 17 more amendments have been added to the Constitution, for a total of 27. For example, the 13th Amendment banned slavery and the 19th Amendment gave women the right to vote. The most recent amendment was added in 1992. It deals with salary changes for members of Congress.

More than 70 years after the states ratified the Bill of Rights, the 14th Amendment was approved. Along with other protections, the 14th Amendment ensures due process and equal protection rights for citizens by the states, too. By itself, the Fifth Amendment only protected those rights for citizens on a federal level. The 14th Amendment extended those rights to the states as well.

KNOW YOUR RIGHTS!

The 27th Amendment was included in the original 12 amendments that were sent to the states to review in 1789. It took more than 200 years to be ratified!

of and ma...

be so construed as to ?egu...

every State in this Union a Republican ? on...

when the Legislature cannot be convened)against domestic v...

Article. V.

of both Houses shall deem it necessary, shall propose Am...

States, shall call a Convention for proposing Amendmen...

ratified by the Legislatures of three fourths of the several S...

by the Congress; Provided that no Amendment which m...

fect the first and fourth Clauses in the Ninth Section of...

the Senate.

Article. VI.

ngagements entered into, before the Adoption of this Const...

deration.

Laws of the United States which shall be made in Pursu...

tes, shall be the supreme Law of the Land; and the Judges...

ontrary notwithstanding.

sentatives before mentioned, and the Members of the several...

al States, shall be bo... ...r Affirmation, to supp...

or public Trust under...

The fifth article of the Constitution explains how new amendments can be proposed and ratified.

Article. VII.

...one States, shall be sufficient for t...

MIRANDA WARNINGS

You may have heard the statements "you have the right to remain silent" and "anything you say can and will be used against you in a court of law" in movies or on television. These are the first two parts of the Miranda warnings, which law enforcement officials are required to recite to citizens who are being arrested.

The Miranda warnings were established after the court case *Miranda v. Arizona* in 1966, when the Supreme Court ruled that individuals must be informed of their rights before being questioned. These warnings are now a standard practice for police when they arrest someone. The warnings inform the person being arrested of their Fifth Amendment rights.

THE RIGHT TO REMAIN SILENT

In the case of *Miranda v. Arizona,* a defendant named Ernesto Miranda confessed to a crime during police questioning. He wasn't informed of his right to remain silent or the right to consult with a lawyer. The court ruled that his Fifth and Sixth Amendment rights were **violated**. As a result of this case, the Miranda warnings were created to clearly explain these rights to suspects.

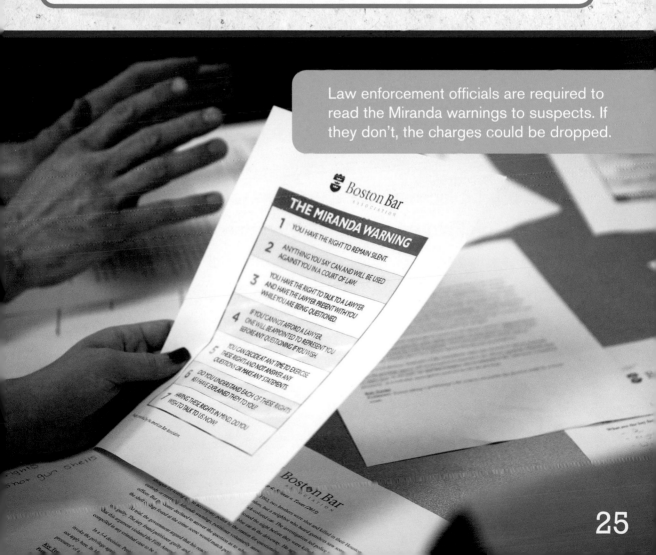

Law enforcement officials are required to read the Miranda warnings to suspects. If they don't, the charges could be dropped.

Boston Bar
ASSOCIATION

THE MIRANDA WARNING

1 YOU HAVE THE RIGHT TO REMAIN SILENT.

2 ANYTHING YOU SAY CAN AND WILL BE USED AGAINST YOU IN A COURT OF LAW.

3 YOU HAVE THE RIGHT TO TALK TO A LAWYER AND HAVE THE LAWYER PRESENT WITH YOU WHILE YOU ARE BEING QUESTIONED.

4 IF YOU CANNOT AFFORD A LAWYER, ONE WILL BE APPOINTED TO REPRESENT YOU BEFORE ANY QUESTIONING IF YOU WISH.

5 YOU CAN DECIDE AT ANY TIME TO EXERCISE THESE RIGHTS AND NOT ANSWER ANY QUESTIONS OR MAKE ANY STATEMENTS.

6 DO YOU UNDERSTAND EACH OF THESE RIGHTS AS I HAVE EXPLAINED THEM TO YOU?

7 HAVING THESE RIGHTS IN MIND, DO YOU WISH TO TALK TO US NOW?

DIFFERENT OPINIONS

There are still disagreements today about how language from the Fifth Amendment should be interpreted. In the 2005 case *Kelo v. City of New London*, the Supreme Court ruled that the government has the right to take over private property and transfer it to another private owner if it will be for public benefit. For example, a new business project could benefit the community by creating jobs, even if the project wouldn't be something for public use like a park or highway.

The court ruled this falls under the "public use" language of the Fifth Amendment. Many people feel this wasn't what the term "public use" meant and believe it's an abuse of the government's eminent domain power.

KNOW YOUR RIGHTS!

After the *Kelo v. City of New London* decision, some states passed laws to prevent this type of situation in the future.

In *Kelo v. City of New London*, the government wanted to take over Susette Kelo's house, as well as some of her neighbors' houses, in New London, Connecticut.

NOT FOR SALE
www.IJ.org

KEEPING UP WITH TECHNOLOGY

Society has changed a lot over the last two centuries, and it's important that our laws keep up. New situations arise that make people question certain parts of the Bill of Rights. It's the Supreme Court's job to help interpret these situations and how they apply to the promises made in the Bill of Rights.

For example, one question in federal courts today is how to handle data privacy in criminal cases. Judges disagree about whether Fifth Amendment rights are violated if suspects are required to give the password for their computer or cell phone. The devices could hold incriminating evidence, and by giving the password, defendants could be providing evidence against themselves.

A judge can order suspects to provide their cell phones or computers as evidence. If the device is locked, law enforcement officials may not be able to log in to get the information stored on it.

CHANGES IN TECHNOLOGY

New **technology** has changed the way people protect their devices. In some cases, cell phones and computers may be unlocked with fingerprints and facial recognition. Some courts have argued that ordering a suspect to unlock a cell phone with a fingerprint or look doesn't violate Fifth Amendment rights, unlike a memorized password. This is because the Fifth Amendment protects thoughts and speech but not physical objects.

AN IMPORTANT ROLE

The Bill of Rights continues to play a very important role in the American legal system. Along with the Constitution and Declaration of Independence, it has shaped the history of the country. The Fifth Amendment is important because it protects citizens' individual rights. It also limits the power of the government, especially for people who are accused of a crime.

As American society changes, its courts and citizens will continue to discuss how the Fifth Amendment should be interpreted. One of the government's jobs is to help the legal system function fairly and efficiently. The Fifth Amendment plays a large role in making sure that happens.

GLOSSARY

deprive: To take away what is needed.

document: A formal piece of writing.

indictment: The act of formally accusing someone of a crime.

infamous: Having a bad reputation.

invoke: To appeal to something as an authority for an action.

jeopardy: In danger of something.

militia: A group of people who are not an official part of the armed forces of a country but are trained like soldiers.

presentment: A statement made by a grand jury.

probable cause: A reasonable basis to think a crime has been committed.

prosecution: A legal act of holding a trial against a person accused of a crime.

technology: A method that uses science to solve problems and the tools used to solve those problems.

testimony: A statement made in court by a witness.

verdict: A decision made by a jury.

violate: To fail to respect someone's rights.

INDEX

WEBSITES

Due to the changing nature of Internet links, PowerKids Press has developed an online list of websites related to the subject of this book. This site is updated regularly. Please use this link to access the list: www.powerkidslinks.com/obor/fifth